AZU's Dreams of Vietnam
Ho Chi Minh City

Published in 2007 by
AZU Editions (Thailand) Ltd.
111 SKV Building, 8/Fl
Soi Sansabai, Sukhumvit Soi 36
Klongton, Klongtoey
Bangkok 10110
Thailand

Tel: 66 (0)2 712-4016
Fax: 66 (0)2 661-2894
office@azueditions.com
www.azueditions.com

ISBN 978-974-8136-53-0

Printed in Malaysia

Copyright 2007
AZU Editions (Thailand) Ltd.

All rights reserved. No part of this publication may be reproduced, stored in a retrieval system or transmitted in any form by any means, electronic, mechanical, photocopying, recording or otherwise, without the prior written permission of AZU Editions (Thailand) Ltd. All content, text, illustrations, and photographs in this publication are protected by national and international trademark and copyright laws. Any infringement of the rights of AZU Editions (Thailand) Ltd. may lead to prosecution without warning.

For information about reproduction rights to the photographs in this book, contact AZU Editions (Thailand) Ltd.

Cover: *The classic Hotel de Ville illuminated at night.*

AZU'S DREAMS OF VIETNAM™

Ho Chi Minh City

Photographs by Leon Schadeberg
Text by John Hoskin

AZU

Exuberant
and enterprising in the extreme,

Previous spread: Although the skyline has changed, the Saigon River remains a city focal point.

Left: A popular outlet for fresh produce and consumer goods, Binh Tey Market stands at a busy intersection.

Ho Chi Minh City appears driven by the freewheeling spirit of youth.

Although now Vietnam's largest city, it was settled in significant numbers only in the eighteenth century. Matching this comparative youth is an almost carefree air that likely stems from the place never having to bear for long the burdens of state.

When the French arrived in 1859, the site of Ho Chi Minh City, on the banks of the Saigon River, was little more than a trade settlement and

a single wooden fort. During the ensuing colonial years, what was then known as Saigon assumed the look more of a French provincial town, and only after independence in 1954 did it acquire status as the capital of the Republic of South Vietnam. Such eminence was lost in 1975 when the country was reunified with Hanoi as its capital.

All this accounts for Ho Chi Minh City having a character of its own, as well as a distinct modern-day role as Vietnam's economic powerhouse. The distinction is well summed up by the quip, 'Hanoi lives by the rules; Saigon lives by its wits.' And first impressions are of a city on the go, a place where the commercial spirit is alive and thrives, whether in a newly built office block or at a street stall.

Above left: A rooftop restaurant provides a fine bird's-eye view of downtown Ho Chi Minh City.

Right: In the grounds of the Jade Emperor Pagoda, one of the most colourful in the city.

Revival and renewal are recurring motifs, and it is a striving towards tomorrow rather than a preservation of the past that typifies Ho Chi Minh City. "Its inspiration," wrote Norman Lewis in 1950, "has been purely commercial and it is therefore without folly, fervour or much ostentation." Little has changed since.

The French, however, couldn't resist a little ostentation, and the baroque Hotel de Ville is a sublime curiosity. Equally oddly European, albeit of less exuberant architecture, is Notre Dame Cathedral.

A flavour of the Orient, however, persists in the city's venerable pagodas, with their crusty tiled roofs and courtyards misted by incense smoke and full of exotic statuary. Giac Lam and Jade Emperor pagodas are

both notable sights, as are the several pagodas tucked away behind the bustling narrow streets of Cholon, the old Chinese quarter.

Yet, Ho Chi Minh City largely lacks the monumental, and its appeal derives from the sum of its parts, while the wide streets, originally laid out by the French, and the river frontage afford pleasant prospects.

Beyond the city, excursions lead to strikingly different but equally intriguing sights, variously the products of war, spirituality, and Nature.

Created out of conflict is the amazing subterranean base of Cu Chi where, during the Vietnam War, the Viet Cong literally holed up in an underground system comprising more than 200 kilometres of hand-dug tunnels. By contrast, the Cao Dai cathedral at Tay Ninh is a

Above left: A seven-storey tower enshrining Buddha images dominates the grounds of Vinh Nghiem Pagoda.

Right: North of the city, the cathedral at Tay Ninh is the spiritual heart of the Cao Dai religion.

manifestation of spiritual vision. Founded in 1919 by Vietnamese mystic Ngo Minh Chieu, the Cao Dai faith embraces a melange of beliefs derived principally from Mahayana Buddhism, Confucianism, Taoism, and Christianity, plus a lacing of spiritualism. Weirdly and wonderfully, this confection of faiths and philosophies is paralleled by the glorious Disney-esque architecture of the Tay Ninh Cathedral.

But it is Nature that has produced the most wondrous sight beyond the city. This is the Mekong Delta, from the air appearing as a great flat greenness threaded with the silver tracery of myriad streams and canals. Thrusting through it all, two huge brown riverine arms impart a muscular feel to a hauntingly primeval landscape.

Above left: Dai Giac Pagoda recalls a Chinese temple in its elaborate interior.

Right: Off the main thoroughfares, quiet side streets retain a tranquil air.

Left: Exploring the Mekong Delta offers a thrilling excursion from the city.

Following spread: Ho Chi Minh City's skyline has changed dramatically in recent years as Vietnam consolidates its economic revival.

Down at water level, the scene seems scarcely less timeless. Thick walls of nipa palms line the banks of streams and creeks, and villages are separated more effectively by dense vegetation than by distance. Only at the junctions of main canals – traditional venues for colourful floating markets – and in the towns that serve the rural communities does human activity momentarily overshadow dominant Nature.

Here, spread over some 970,000 hectares of Vietnam's southernmost tip, is one of the last tourism frontiers in Southeast Asia.

Above: *In spite of modern development, Notre Dame Cathedral remains a prominent landmark.*

Right: *Distinctive among the city's new landmarks is the HSBC bank building.*

Above: The classic Hotel Continental continues to rank among the top accommodation options.

Right: Completed in 1891, the Central Post Office is designed in grand colonial style.

Left: *Students dressed in their traditional white ao dais leave class for the day.*

Above: *The grandiose Municipal Theatre, first opened in 1899, blends the classical with the colonial.*

Previous spread: *Reunification Hall is built on the site of the former residence of the French governor-general.*

Left: *Fanciful architecture at the Cao Dai cathedral in Tay Ninh.* ***Above:*** *An orchestra accompanies prayers inside the cathedral.*

Above: *The 'Divine Eye' is the official symbol of the Cao Dai religion, reputedly appearing to the sect's founder in a vision.*

Right: *Noon prayers amid the extraordinary interior of the faith's cathedral at Tay Ninh.*

Following spread: *Changing times: a statue of Ho Chi Minh stands in front of the colonial-era Hotel de Ville.*

Above: *A devotee burns incense before praying at the Jade Emperor Pagoda.*

Right: *Chua Ong Pagoda is classically Chinese in its religious architecture.*

Above: *The peaceful cloisters of Ha Chuang Pagoda is the place to enjoy tea and quiet moments.*

Right: *At prayer in Quan Am Pagoda, where burning coils of incense are suspended from the roof.*

Above: *Fashions of today and yesterday meet on a bridge over the lake at Dam Sen Park.*

Right: *Dam Sen Park's lake sports fanciful statuary in front of a Chinese tea house.*

Following spread: *Morning exercises, Chinese style, at Tao Dan Park.*

Above: The cyclo, a slow but sure way of getting through the traffic. **Right:** Bicycles are ubiquitous, but motorcycles are fast catching up in numbers.

Following spread: Shoppers browse around the fresh produce stalls of Bachieu Market.

Left: *Coconut milk is a refreshing streetside buy in the heat of the day.*

Above: *Vendors await customers at their stall offering fresh baguettes with delicious fillings.*

Above and right: *The statue of Tran Hung Dao honours the thirteenth-century warrior, a brother of the king of the ruling Tran Dynasty, who achieved a brilliant victory over the superior forces of Kublai Khan.*

Above: *A ferry crosses the Saigon River, with the high-rises of downtown Ho Chi Minh City in the background.*

Right: *A more traditional scene prevails on the opposite bank of the river from the city centre.*

Above and right:
River craft, large and small, ply the waterways of the Mekong Delta, where myriad streams and canals thread their way between banks of dense vegetation to connect with the main river.

Above and right:
Traditional performances at the Bongsen Theatre.

Following spread:
The spacious downtown streets clearly display the city planning of the colonial era.

Ho Chi Minh City

Travel Facts

Where It Is

Ho Chi Minh City is in the southeast corner of Vietnam on the banks of the Saigon River, about twenty kilometres from the coast. It lies just east of the vast Mekong Delta region and is 1,760 kilometres south of the capital Hanoi. Its geographical coordinates are 10 degrees North, 106 degrees East.

How To Get There

By Air
Tan Son Nhat International Airport is Vietnam's main air hub, through which most visitors to the country will arrive. It is located seven kilometres north of the city and is served by an increasing number of direct international and domestic flights. There are also numerous options for connections via Bangkok, Singapore, and Hong Kong.

By Train
Ho Chi Minh City is the main terminus of the Trans-Vietnam Railroad, which runs parallel to the coast to Hanoi and on to the Chinese border about 1,950 kilometres to the north. The train station is northwest of the city centre.

By Road
The city is easily accessible by road from many places in southern Vietnam. National Highways provide links to the Mekong Delta region, the Central Highlands, the Central Coast region, and the north. Two expressways will run to Can Tho, the capital of the Delta, and to Dau Giay, seventy kilometres to the northeast. There are also regular bus services to Cambodia and Laos.

When To Go

Ho Chi Minh City has a tropical climate, with the level of humidity (averaging 75 percent) exacerbated by its proximity to the sea. There are two main seasons – wet and dry – but it remains hot throughout the year, with temperatures ranging from 28 to 39 degrees Celsius, although it may fall to as low as 16 degrees Celsius in the early mornings of the dry season.

The dry season generally lasts from December to April, during which time average temperatures may be cooler. Rains start in May and become heavy from June to August, but the showers are mostly sudden and short-lived.

Average annual rainfall is 1,800 mm and there are about 100 rainy days per year. Typhoons are a risk from July to November.

The best time to visit is in the dry season between December and April, when the humidity is not so oppressive. Between November and March the number of visitors tends to increase, while the Tet festival in late January or early February is an exciting but extremely busy national holiday.

Find Out More

Comprehensive information for visitors can be found at the Vietnam National Administration of Tourism's excellent website **www.vietnamtourism.gov.vn**. For more general information go to **www.vietnamtourism-info.com/english** or **www.hochiminhcity.gov.vn/eng.**

Above: *A flower vendor offers blooms for sale on a typical city street.*

Acknowledgements

The publisher would like to thank the following whose assistance has made this book possible:

Ramita Saisuwan and Keith Hardy.

Authors

Leon Schadeberg is a British photographer who has been based in Southeast Asia since 1990. He has travelled extensively throughout the region documenting culture, travel, and lifestyle. His work has been exhibited frequently, both locally and internationally.

John Hoskin is an award-winning freelance travel writer who has been based in Thailand since 1979. He is the author of many highly acclaimed books on travel, art, and culture in Southeast Asia, and has had over 1,000 magazine articles published.